POETRY AN'
Sleeping
with the
Secret
Burden

by

Dee Alimi

Copyright © 2013 Dee Alimi

All rights reserved.

ISBN: 148020319X
ISBN-13: 9781480203198

LCCN: 2012920557
CreateSpace Independent Publishing Platform,
North Charleston, South Carolina

Dedicated to my mother.

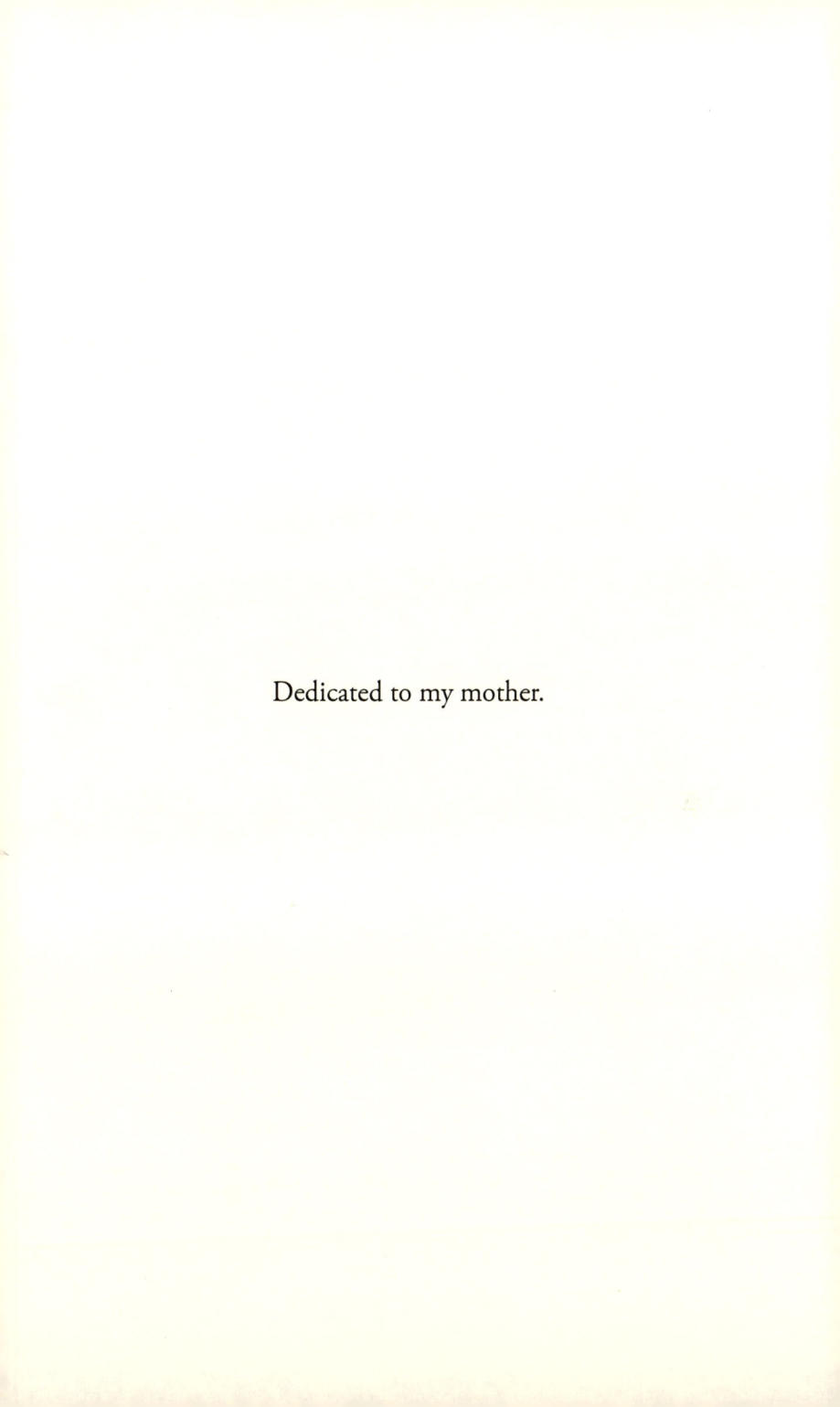

Review

Alimi's debut poetry collection marks the milestones of an emotional journey of self-exploration across Europe and Africa.

In this multifaceted work, Alimi offers a variety of poems about how he perceives his own life, love and the women who captivate him. …The author explains that he used the poems to help him understand his own personal setbacks and move on with his life. …The poems are grouped into nine chapters, and many share the themes of infatuation and doomed romance. …The collection tells the story of Alimi's emotional development, but the author is fully capable of writing from other points of view; one poem that demonstrates this, "Diana," begins, "Beautiful red dress looks sunkissed," and soon shifts to deeper concerns: "I'm so fed up, all I tried was to be someone. At times self-respect is far from my mind." …At one point, when the verses turn away from soft skin and sweet lips, they compare a relationship to a game of chess.

An intriguing collection about overcoming obstacles and finding inner peace …

Kirkus Reviews

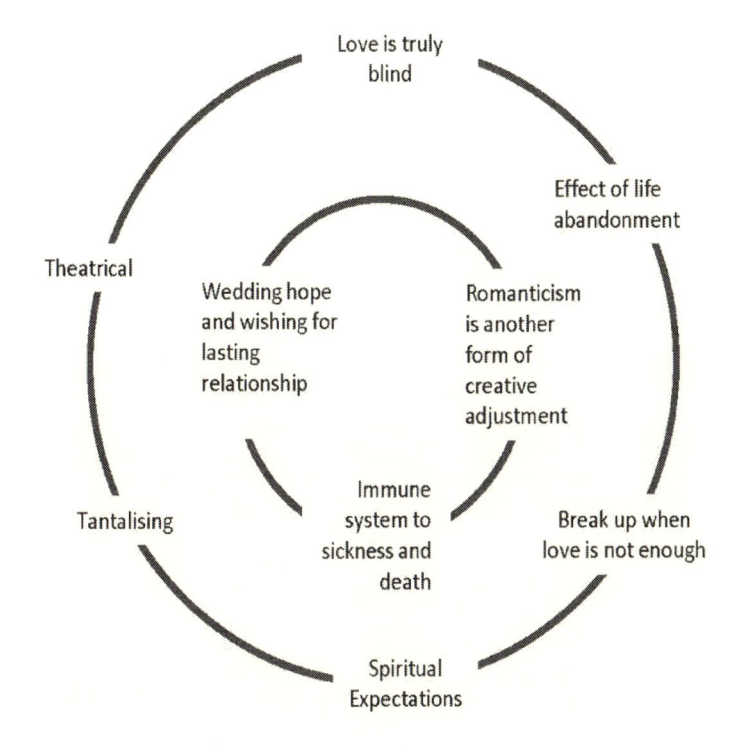

- Love is truly blind
- Effect of life abandonment
- Theatrical
- Wedding hope and wishing for lasting relationship
- Romanticism is another form of creative adjustment
- Tantalising
- Immune system to sickness and death
- Break up when love is not enough
- Spiritual Expectations

Poetry Theme

Preface

I used to receive love letters and cards from an ex-girlfriend whilst at University. Much later I wrote my first poem for someone that I wanted to be with. She had some sort of skin cancer. Although it was treated, I didn't know what to do in that moment as my heart poured out. I wrote a poem on the back of my business card and gave it to her when I was working in Genoa, Italy on contract. It was in Italy that I discovered Spiritualism.

I thought: what would it take to be with her? It was that longing for her affection that drove me to write passionate poems. Since then I have enjoyed writing about different subjects and themes.

The poems are a range of romanticism, places I have visited, earth-bound, relationships, grief, and human injustice. The latter is the reason why this book is called 'Sleeping with the Secret Burden', after an article I had read in one of the broadsheet newspapers. I was touched by the story, and still am to this day. Some poems were written because I draw from my life's failures to date and wonder what could have been. But it's in these failures that I have found the strength and courage to shift; to embark on a journey of writing poems and prose to keep my innermost beacon of hope alive – to be aware of what I am, rather than what could be.

Table of Contents

Chapter One
Break Up When Love Is Not Enough   1

Forever My Lady	2
Immaculate Sorrow	3
Macedonia	4
Painful Love	7
Broken Heart	8
Taste of Love	10

Chapter Two
Romanticism Is Another Form Of Creative Adjustment   11

Second Time	12
To Be Loved	14
Cheeky Star	15
Foolish Love	16
Driven Eyes	17
Obsession	18
Affection	19
Out Of Nowhere	20
No Idea	22

Smile 22
Empathy 23
Honey 24
Pagoda 24

Chapter Three
Theatrical **25**

Dark Longing 26
India Lost 4 Words 27
Endless 28

Chapter Four
Wedding Hope And Wishing For
Lasting Friendship **29**

Could You Be The one? 30
I Can't Believe It 31

Chapter Five
Spiritual Expectations **33**

Gandhi 34
Alzheimer's Body 36
Making Up 37
Diana 39
Heaven Summit On Earth 41

Spreading Wings 43
Planet In Confusion 45
Hero From Distance 46
Low Volume 47
Hungarian Flower 48
Many Eyes 49
Autumn Falling Leaves 50
Rain 50
Lonely Galaxy 51

Chapter Six
Effect Of Life Abandonment 53

Secret Burden 54
Living Water 56
Frida De Aba 57
First Encounter 60
Missing Peace 61

Chapter Seven
Tantalising 63

Llamada Cachonda Part 1 64
Llamada Cachonda (Mexico- Booty call) 65

Chapter Eight
Love Is Truly Blind 67

Closer Moment	68
M25 Romantic Jammin	69
Violeta	71
Beauty Of Monterrey	71
Romantic Tale of Afreurop	72
Exercise	73
Maria	73
Neuchatel Lake	74
La Mia Stanzetta (My Room)	75
Taiwanese Hero	76
Un Bel Posto (Beautiful Place)	77
Damascus	78

Chapter Nine
Immune System To Sickness And Death   79

Smiling Soul	80
Battling With Hay Fever	81
Cancer Season	83

Acknowledgments

I thank Devine Beings for their ineffable love. I would like to thank my editor Jacquie Buttriss and friends (including Samina Yasmeen) and family members that have supported me over the years.

Chapter One

Break Up When Love Is Not Enough

Forever My Lady

Will you ever return to me?

Do you ever think of me as I thought of you?

Do I ever cross your mind to behold your love for me?

Ever since you've gone, I forever hold you in my thoughts.

Whatever possessed me to let you go?

Forever green you are in my eyes,

Forever I will love you,

Forever I will share our sentimental memories of togetherness.

We will be forever in our hearts of magical tenderness, dusted with ashes.

Forever I await you not.

Immaculate Sorrow

Today, I saw you in all glory of beauty; attraction captured my luminous eyes.

There you turn a corner, with love that saddens your hidden plight.

Our emotional connection erupts like a love waiting, in execution.

No amount of sorrows could grieve this sadness; I see it now.

It erases all hurt, fear, revenge, ambivalence and sets me free with oneness, openness.

Macedonia

You told me of your wedding day,

Only two days to go,

Destroyed my mind became,

My heart tumbled and fell beneath guilt,

My selfish emotions immersed me.

I blamed myself for pushing you away to marry another,

Knowing that I will always be in your heart.

Your husband to be will always be second.

I too will become second to as time passes.

You gave me all your love, but I know that my mind doesn't want you for you;

All of me is complex and perfected to the point of fallacy,

But you showed me what it means to love without prejudice.

You erase my hurts and the heartache of distant pain.

I thank you, as your love is the true love'

I believe that you loved me for me,

You gave up your life just to be with me,

And I betrayed you with hurt.

I acted foolishly, like an immature player,

But you gave me time to see things your way.

I was too wrapped up with a tasteless apple.

I honestly believe that we will never be,

But love is powerful.

You're like a butterfly that yields honey upon my lips,

You brightened up my days with your words of courage and wisdom,

You displayed hunger for knowledge.

You respected and treated me like a king as you looked up to me.

You gave up your past and present just because you loved me,

I was so scared to adopt you.

I have been wrong on many occasions.

However, opportunities are never the same way.

If I were to follow what goes around comes around,

The price would be over-inflated with pain of a tasteless apple.

Soon I will leave the one I currently love,

And solo I will remain until the time I find someone else.

All I want now is to be alone, until I rediscover my true self and reflect on the hurts caused

Because I feel so shameful for how I treated you.

I'm so sorry,

I know that I can never say sorry enough to erase the pain and hurt.

I can never have your Macedonia.

I pledge to change my ways and be good to my next love.

Please forgive me.

Tears fall as I conclude this poem,

Because I feel that I drove you to marrying.

I know you don't want this

But I left you no choice.

You returned to Macedonia to seek refuge, salvation and heal the wounds.

I could not imagine the magnitude of hurt that I caused you and how it came to this.

I love you Macedonia,

This is why I'm hurting inside,

And I know you love me too,

I decided to let you have your peace and enjoy new, true love.

Let the flame burn out and rekindle with friendship.

Forever, I will always love you.

Painful Love

Oh foxy baby, devilish are your eyes, filled with secrecy.

Your presence burns a flame of promiscuity.

Infatuation casts wonders over my eyelids.

Thought of entangling danger crosses my mind.

Humorous, challenging it seems to unravel depths of unfaithfulness.

Passion waits no longer for thy act of folly.

Spare of moments of lust or fancy,

Pain befalls my heart,

Cruel and humiliated by eyes of witnesses.

Broken Heart

Sadly you told me you no longer want me.

I begged you to stay with me for a time.

I drown in my tears.

If I lose you now, I've lost the centre of my life.

Crumbling, my life became ruined beyond repair,

Although a broken heart can be mended, but the scar lives on.

I called you many times, hoping for your return.

You tell me let's be friends.

It's not enough as you wanted what's truly yours.

I ignored your plea and became stubborn.

I sometimes miss you so much, but it's too hard to let you know what I feel,

Knowing that you want me so much.

I'm so sure news of my loneliness spread.

I became a target for those who seek material love.

My mind remains with one I love.

I stand with many, but my heart relives the wonderful moments,

My eyes wonder through the growth of life,

I had to change wind direction,

I became stronger through my pain,

I am weakened when you're near for your love is breathtaking.

I always feel you in my mind, even though we're apart.

I too, feel guilty of letting you go.

Now I return to a nest that's always mine and forever to stay.

Taste of Love

Infatuation seems young;

An emotional feeling that confuses adults.

It fails to feed my hungry belly

For your thoughts drench my selfishness.

How unkind love can be at times.

Heart hurts so badly and broken like a shellfish;

I have no remedy except time.

Lingering anguish of bitterness unleashed.

I ask you to look at good times and invite laughter.

I know bad times remain yesterday;

Understand the purpose of this love.

Love is blind, love is kind, love is graceful and love is forgiven;

Grow love and let it be your power beyond infinity.

Chapter Two

*Romanticism Is Another Form Of Creative Adjustment**

---

*Perls, Frederick, Ralph F. Hefferline, & Paul Goodman. Gestalt Therapy

Second Time

In my delight of your presence

I hide my face in darkness.

You wonder close to my heartbeat,

Sounds of a volcano in love.

I see only glitz of your glamour.

The world flocks to you and reacts effortlessly,

Like a bird tendering her chick.

I watch from a distance.

Though my uncertainty weans upon my emotions,

You shine like stars.

Your radiant beauty like the sun on Jupiter

And mesmerise in reflection of Mars.

Behold – in this illustrious beauty comes the dazzling smile

That melts all hearts and sets itself motionless in a realm of heavens

And above darkness.

Our memory of night blooms blossomy,

So grand,

So beautiful,

So energetic and magnetic.

Thus I remain your secret admirer, longing to be forever yours.

To Be Loved

How do I mean to love you?

How do you see love?

How do you feel love?

How do you sense true love of romance?

How can I tell you I love you when you doubt yourself?

How can my love mean something to you?

Superficial eyes lay beneath negativity,

I have no remedy to change your heart.

However, I do possess the charm to excavate the reasoning of your mind

without pain, there's no hope in waiting for true love.

Love expresses itself in many ways.

I do not doubt your anger of emotion, locked in between.

Look a little deeper and see the flame of love that carries you through thick & thin.

Love with single happiness serves no purpose for humanity.

Although my love is contradictory, no words could describe my motion of feelings for you.

Life is love, but life is greater than love.

Cheeky Star

Cloudy marques in crowded places,

There you are, lost within the mist of hazy sunshine.

I gaze through the light that shines through the vent.

My brown eyes blink for your attention.

Though you look on like a flower opening its petals,

Like pebbles on the beach you stroll gently into sea.

Swan and Dove are no match for your beauty.

Oh how heavenly you sway among the beeches,

You are my cheeky star.

Foolish Love

So nervous I was when you were near,

I began to unwind my emotions.

Your touch was remarkably sensitive;

I yearn for your touch,

Holding hands, sharing tensions of anxiety,

Although you sat peacefully, many thoughts ponder,

Your cuddle so heartfelt.

Your voice is like sweet melody to my ears,

Your smile glows, your ivory of nature,

Your hair smooth like rose of Galilee;

So much to admire.

Your strength, inner courage, trust and above all – wisdom of life.

Wishful thinking casts a shadow as I yearn for your wholeness.

I cause no harm to our lasting friendship;

I pray to dare not lose a friend but to embark on a beautiful journey of everlasting romance.

Driven Eyes

Striving heart beat softens,

Emotion mingling with intuition,

Feelings that is invisible to many eyes,

Eyes overwhelmed by others' unconditional love,

Sacrifices with choice of freedom,

In whose eyes judgement should pass,

Whirl round like a wheel of fortune.

Human race drifts far from compassion,

Although your sincerity lives within many;

Let not your ego or pride stand in way of love.

 I ask, what do you have to lose?

OBSESSION

Driven into anger of frustration,

Your thoughts of reasoning fade like stardust.

Intelligence of unruly nature sets in.

How I trusted you, for I loved so....

You showed me the dark side of your love.

Realisation of loneliness captures my mind,

Sooner must I find true love of my heart.

In fear I live life because of you.

I became paranoid without knowing,

Although I pretended to have loved,

But I love another, alone I mesmerise romance of honesty.

I wished so many things remained the same;

How naive love can be.

On the whole I humble my principle of love.

AFFECTION

So much I shared my loving feelings,

But guarded with iron bar of melted facets.

I see so many characteristics in all,

But not all confined within a woman.

I search for many qualities that my mind and heart seeks.

I awake from dreamland;

Dreamless mind fantasises many beauties.

Confused it may look like, for whom?

My heart will not rest until it's naturally satisfied - wholeness of my other half.

Out Of Nowhere

I don't know why I feel to write this poem;

My emotions ride me like the love I have for you,

Although thought of the past reminisces through me.

We met in a club with superficial views.

I wanted to love you and you to love me.

You decided not to love at first.

I painted a picture of peace and tarnished it with romance of my lifetime.

You told me you could not love.

But love is like flower-buds that flourish during spring.

I too played my part to see how minds can be put under romantic spell.

I pushed you to surrender into my arms, but not of physical desire - you didn't understand.

So, you turned it into a game of chess.

You never thought about your opponent's past skills.

I am as humble as the wind that blows through the lake at dawn,

Please forgive me if you feel that I played you; it's not my intention.

I have so much love to give those who are in search of everlasting love, but not to those materially minded.

My past experience has no part to play in this love; I choose to love all races equally.

I know you are long gone to your country, and I will miss you so much.

You understand little of me because I view the world with an open mind.

I take the opportunity to thank my higher state of consciousness for its grace and kindness.

I owe you so much, but not even one grain of sand of this world can equal the debt of love.

You've set me free, like a colourful butterfly nurturing the flowers of the earth.

I rest my weary soul upon you for peace and honesty.

No Idea

So softly you look,

Your tender eyes express innocence.

How can I not love you?

You're the apple-berry of my eyes.

You told me "don't say you love me".

What we feel at times doesn't equal words,

For these feelings are beyond the imagination of humankind.

I tell you today - I love you with my heart and mind.

Smile

Your smile is like a wave, rippling across the sea shore.

Golden sand dusts your soft skin,

Light brown stones camouflage your complexion,

But your eyes, visible like sun setting from a distance,

Your teeth reflect the shadow of planet earth.

EMPATHY

What's within my root at times reveals not why I endure.

My endurance is penetrated deeper in the sea water,

Filtering the surrounding sand and rocks.

I yearn for the wind, the star, the moon and the sun,

But the sea surface looks blurred. Why?

I decide to grow in harmony by sharing my wonderful thoughts with the lily flower,

Hoping it will embrace me with peace, courage, love and laughter.

Now, I thank the lily for its fulfilment and the joy it brings me seems never ending.

Honey

Yet another day filled with thoughts of you;

I wait in anticipation to be at your side,

A stranger yearning for togetherness.

You're the rock that holds me up when I'm falling,

You're the honey that sweetens my lips.

Pagoda

Pretty, cute, beauty,

How glamorous you look when you're near,

Your touch sends roaring sea waves down my spine,

Your lips are as sweet as cherries,

Your eyes are dusted with tenderness.

My mind is inspired with thoughts not of this world.

Chapter Three

Theatrical

Dark Longing

She writes in the season of love.

Beneath her is the curious ground

Where bears lie in muddy waters.

O handsome one, are you there?

I have lost the one I love.

Midst of fury cast over me,

Shadows of death give rise to worthlessness.

O handsome one, are you there?

A woman without her beloved, perished in anguish.

Distress in breath, her heart corroded,

Corrosion of dark illusion.

O handsome one, are you there?

She writes in the season of love,

Sings in the season of sadness,

Weeps in anger,

Awakes the angels of heavens,

Silently whispers:

O handsome one, are you there?

India Lost 4 Words

Look! The sun is behind you.

Ah, I'm your beauty of light,

Surrounded by the city of light, replete with angels.

Down on my knees, the sun blasts my face with warmth,

Smiles rise to my cheeks.

I'm beautiful because I glow richer than the stars.

I'm blossom because my mind is like the full moon triangle

Ooooooh! Nooooo!

Three of me is too much for the world to behold.

I can't explain to you in words;

I'm no artist of words,

I express words with my feelings.

Through your eyes I saw a rainbow looming over me,

So colourful like seasons of love.

My sweet affection goes deeper than you could ever imagine.

No words could portray my emotions for you,

The tantalising moment is beyond infinity.

Endless

How I hate your presence.

I don't understand my attraction,

But I keep on like a flow of ocean falling into erosion.

Beginning seems so peaceful and full of laughter.

How could I trust a stranger with the key of my heart and soul?

This eats me away from your love.

I love you and I can't hate you,

Although bitter it may sound -

Yes, it's sweet bitter love.

The end is an endless love.

Chapter Four

Wedding Hope And Wishing For Lasting Friendship

Could You Be The one?

Could you be the one who holds me up and sweetens my lips?

Could you be the one who holds me when I'm fallen?

Could you be my rock of refuge?

Could you be the love I yearn for day and night?

I search for peaceful love that could breeze my pain of heartache.

My feet rejoice because of your dancing, musical mind.

I rain through the cloud that sees no one but you.

Your radiant smile reflects my world of beauty,

Ivory jewels that shine like silver clouds.

An ivory tower is no match for your elegance.

Petite in style,

Feminine in mind,

With a heart of pure diamond.

I Can't Believe It

Alone I walk the big city with my face down,

Contemplating how should I approach your fragile, lonely heart,

Although you show no sign of weakness to the world,

The eyes cloud with puffs of water waiting to drop silently,

But my pride would not let me be submissive into unknown arms.

If I fell for you like falling autumn leaves, please forgive me,

Because your kindness has over shadowed my prejudiced mind and soul;

You're the light that brightens up my day,

You're the moon that dawn upon my footpath at night,

You're the stars that uplift me from the heap of ashes and settle the dust upon the precious valley.

Chapter Five

Spiritual Expectations

GANDHI

Determination prevails,

Violence serves no justice for freedom,

Peace is far from the human soul,

Greed and selfish interest rules the world.

I'm not bitter.

I hopelessly deepen in sorrows to my heart's content,

I can bear it no longer,

I offer my words of wisdom.

I gave up my life for the freedom of those to come.

Senseless behaviour draws the tension of aggression;

I adopted a little child of different race and colour,

Who treated me like a father, and I treated my child like my own.

Tolerance springs to mind;

Loving another person's child as your own is an act of love and compassion.

Words of wisdom that brought tears to the eyes of many are those that remind us of the meaning of humanity.

Neglect of childhood reminisces through the world of kindness and hatred.

Vision forms the suffering of physical and mental depression,

Although, depression is a form of loneliness.

Cry no more and look around you,

Angels dance among you.

Reach out your hands so they are touched with warmth and gentleness.

Through emotional anger and mental pain I have learnt to live without fear.

Alzheimer's Body

Too little time we give this precious dwelling,

Mysterious in many dimensions of composition;

Not one part of me is alone.

Dead skin flakes off and renews itself, because of its nature;

What seems perfect in one's eyes can cause delusion of anger,

Anger towards whom, I ask?

I have no right to be angry;

All I have inside is love,

Your love that rains upon me like that of forest showers,

You compelling, my heart and mind couldn't contain.

In so many ways, you've made the perfect house,

But its contents are too wonderful.

Although many are unfortunate, not of their of own will but of lack.

I wish for warmth and comfort to be still within those missing dwellings, with misguided thoughts.

I conclude this writing with honesty and integrity.

Making Up

I feel so much to love many girls of all races,

My selfish desire is of feelings of loneliness,

Sharing one of the world's most beautiful creations,

Girls, girls, girls;

I love you all,

But the time has come to do away with self-interest,

And bring those children of divinity nearer.

I'm confused as I imagine fading dreams,

I rally myself with prayers,

Meditation is food for thought,

I contemplate on the communication of the small still voice within.

Angels watch over me,

Reminding me of the object of desire,

They embrace me with all my flaws.

I'm so unhappy with my recent past,

I know what I'm capable of and know others are just as good as me.

In the end I have to give in and surrender to my purpose in existing.

The bigger picture reappears, showing me the way to go.

Although I have burdened you with my trouble, you never left my side,

And I'm grateful to you all.

May the kiss of peace find you and enlighten the eyes of my heart.

DIANA

Beautiful red dress looks sunkissed.

Solo, I travel many places,

Yearning for survival.

Those who surround honour liberties.

I'm so fed up, all I tried was to be someone.

At times self-respect is far from my mind.

I feel my mind rusting and falling into arms of the low-minded,

My heart pounds in agony asking where are you when I need you,

But who am I to ask?

My optimism and faith lead to alleyways of brightness

I read only the lips of those who face me.

Nature gives up itself.

I challenge my heart with fear.

I decide to dance - for rhythm far too deep to hold,

Burst onto the stage floor, living a dream.

Life gives a second chance.

Love flows from this moment on,

Compassion with true love fly together like a skeleton wave beneath the sky,

How challenging is life without a quantum leap.

Heaven Summit On Earth

So many passed away through sadness, no fault of their own.

How can we replace those we love and who loved us?

Their love is irreplaceable.

Although the little things you do to annoy me suddenly become unimportant,

I wish the days of laughter could return.

I await your hugs and kisses,

If you only let me touch you.

I promise to cleanse my undevoted thoughts before you;

Devoted you imagine them to be,

For you're the one lovin' me without judgement,

You're the one flooding my past with distant memories,

You're the one saturating my heart,

Fading into unknown spiral self.

How guilty I'm feeling as your shadows overlay my pathway.

I know I cannot turn back the clock,

But I forgive you as your eyes widen,

Your experience causes you to love unconditionally.

The pain you endured was to make you understand the meanin' of life and to rejoice in the charity of everlasting.

I blame not my chosen lifestyle.

I spread my grace upon those who walk in kindness and merciful heart;

In abundance I welcome you into my arms without burden.

Spreading Wings

All week I feel so sad and lonely,

Thinking you're far from me.

I reminisce on the good times.

Suddenly I forget how you used to correct me.

Now I'm tearful with joy;

You turn my sadness into happiness.

Spiritually and emotionally I yearn for your comfort.

You pass-me-by like a breeze from the wind.

Through missing you I have learnt to love and let go of my anger of the past.

You're closer to me than the hair of my skin.

Smile overshadows my face.

Twinkling eyes light like heaven's door.

There you are standing with angels.

How can I be with you?

I fall to my feet.

I repent and promise myself to do good.

Your gentleness overwhelms my heart.

Your shadow, your words become the footpath of my life.

I deepen to touch you but you respond with warmth.

I thank you for loving me without judgment.

The rain washes my sorrows away and I fly away free as a butterfly.

Planet In Confusion

Sound with bang,

Lightning blitzes through the blue sky,

Inside catches flame of mysterious beauty,

Wet it looks from a distance,

Cloudiness draws closer,

The earth plate awakens itself,

Fragmented ground below sea level forces the sea kingdom to escape through narrow waves.

Hero From Distance

Slowly I watched a shooting star at the brink, on her knees,

Destined for wholeness of equality.

World cannot accept the truth,

Although I play no part on either side.

Loving memories of spoken words that could not translate into reality live within many hearts.

Statue of a great hero to some and, for others, dust is more comforting than ashes at large.

Their legacy will hunt those who suppress the common good of all.

No wind blows without sound and no soul travels without consciousness.

Low Volume

Lonely I felt after many days of togetherness.

Decision made by natural lack of harmony,

Although I did not want you to leave because of my selfish way.

Mind intervenes and heart withers in agony, but intellect prevails,

Sickness immersed me and my innermost strength,

Adding to unfocused love, desperate to sleep the broken peace.

Hungarian Flower

Oh, young child filled with hopes and joy to come,

Happiness of moment which does not equal lifetime growth, causing delusion.

Protected I am until loops of small waves intoxicate my fragile tube.

Season of endurance and rebirth springs to mind.

My heights and depths often seduced me from the reality of engagement.

Mind of young lily flower falls without hope of defence.

I wish this lily hadn't fallen,

But whatever happens you will always be my Hungarian flower.

MANY EYES

So I can't begin to understand this love, and feelings I have inside.

Your beauty is everywhere, this is beyond comprehension for eyes and mind;

You're closer to me than the hair on my skin.

How can I return this debt of love?

Although I thank you in so many little ways, but even all the grains of sand of this world cannot equal your kindness and compassion.

You ask nothing of me in return, but if only the rest were alike.

Now, I rest myself on your caring thoughts.

This writing instrument cannot put into words the deeper feelings, shared without favouritism.

In so many ways you've made my feet firm on the ground, a solid foundation.

Autumn Falling Leaves

Withered leaves fall without prejudice,

Harsh leaves travel into wind and scatter like star butterflies,

Beautiful, brown, curly skin, rich in kindness and compassion.

Leaves grow, leaves fall, leaves reveal their colourful nature,

Roots penetrating and saturating the ground with unconditional love,

Wholeness of universe, mulberry tree leaves fall short of my love for you.

Rain

Once more the air I breathe is cleansed,

Rain freely falls out of the sky without prejudice.

Universes of flowers celebrate and embrace the love of mysterious nature.

Underground creatures inter-mingle and intertwine

Praise freely given with love and compassion.

Lonely Galaxy

Tree stems bow, sea waves roar, Saharan dust blows into the sky,

Stars darken through the eye of cloudiness,

Moon shines restlessly with sorrow,

Sun rises from east and desperate waters evaporate.

Children play together, unconscious of the world's discrimination.

Little can we do to rescue mother nature from the world's depravation.

From within, tear drops feeling the anguish of nature,

Peaceful, joyful, graceful; I hear the children yearn and seek with whole hearts,

Trembling grounds, mountains, valleys and lakes; feel pure compassion.

Rainbow surrounds thy loving children, like feather wings upon beautiful white doves.

Chapter Six

Effect Of Life Abandonment

Secret Burden

Silent, I weep in sorrow.

Inside of me is incurable;

Society will not understand,

Neither the ones who are close to me

Because their minds are hypnotised by worldly attributes

Solo I set out, not wanting to burden another.

This load breaks my heart, knowing that I'm still here,

But for what?!

To withdraw from the universe, confined to my imagination,

My weakened heart will perish like a cliff falling into sea,

Decay like melted snow water.

I suffer alone, though much of this has nothing to do with me.

I suffer inherited pain,

I sleep and wake in terror of tomorrow;

Through my emotion I have learned many compassionate words,

Words that help me look forward to a brighter day, as stars belong to the sky at night

I consider myself lucky as many more are just like me, afar from kindness,

With neglect not of their own willingness,

I dream of freedom, as a butterfly intoxicates those like me with peace.

Beyond infinity is my love for you,

Night and day I hope you find relief from misery,

Despair not of bitterness but of grace,

Let your heart be your rock of refuge and your fortress.

Living Water

It sounds so easy when I tell about past

Memories of neglect, bringing tears to my eyes,

I blame no one, nor those that gave birth to me.

Through my experience I learnt to understand many troubles of others.

I can't tell why I'm to go through life this way,

But my past helps others just as it has shaped my thoughts and reasoning

I hold no grudges against those who are meant to be responsible;

They too have their own life to lead,

Like a child lost in desert lands,

I weaken inside; yet somehow you strengthen me to strive forward.

Daily you remind me of my object of desire

I'm to be whatever I choose, but not of selfish interest or revenge.

Continue to love all living creatures and peace will find you.

From my innermost heart I thank those I've met along my path of life so far.

I look forward to another day because best of times are yet to come.

Frida De Aba

I'm a child with a sense of curiosity;

I ponder on what made the enemy tick in mind.

I was the curiosity that killed the cat, but not the Cheshire cat.

I became a mother with no hope, imbued with mistrust.

My life is smoother, like rain that's forever whingeing.

In affection caught me and spared the death of me.

My beautiful girl is left alone;

I will watch over you with my brightest eyes.

I am so sorry my little girl,

May God bless you beyond your wildest dream,

I whisper silently, sorrow looming over me.

Grandmother shows me love more than my own mother could,

Because she is no more.

If I was born to suffer in life, then why was I born?

If fate has surpassed me, then destiny awaits my ending.

It was not by choice that I was born of misfortune,

However the wheel of fortune turns,

I am the face of the nation, with fame that causes sadness.

I just can't be me, because my life will be like breadcrumbs that fall on a dog's mouth.

I am savage alone, and alone I weep in agony.

My pain has grown to defeat my little memory of joy.

I too lost a small child of my own.

I count the price of fate.

I discount the joy that shields my past fears.

Oh mama, I am so ashamed for me, not for you because you're my mother.

I can't change you, neither my own past.

I thank you for your best, although it wasn't good enough.

I poured out my best for love to rain over me.

I feel so cold and lacking hate.

I'm eaten up inside by depression.

I was found by my lost father,

Although bitterness shed with tears is a sense of confinement.

Now, I am more popular than you could ever imagine.

However, I'm still unhappy because I am your little girl.

I have lost and found and lost.

I hope to find a resting place with you, mama,

Because my life is a secret burden.

First Encounter

One reveals one's inner affection without thought,

The eyes wander, gazing at nature's best beauty and desire.

This nature is no other than your shadow,

Searching for the peace, harmony, togetherness and tranquillity at first sight,

But who am I to seek your mind?

Missing Peace

How cruel is the world from outside,

Quick to judge without thought,

Mind of mice;

Even mice have greater inner sustenance.

Speak not with thy artificial vision.

Let your mind glow and radiate the energy of passion,

Love of such, grows like seeds scattered beneath the clay soil.

Nourish your soil with light and positive vibration.

Now, the seed flourish was like that of the Garden of Eden.

Chapter Seven

Tantalising

Llamada Cachonda Part 1

Many sweet voices call me,

Screaming out for passion of excavation,

And only I possess the key to unlock the graveness.

I pinpoint my target, covered in grass of human hair,

Of brown, ginger, dark, yellow colours but not of greenfield,

Curly and straight, they appear,

But the attraction to penetrate the skin overwhelms my desire,

Hoping your fingers will reach my hottest spot,

Water down my breath reminisces kissing game.

LLAMADA CACHONDA (MEXICO- BOOTY CALL)

Talking over a piece of string leads to temptation,

String that fills a precious gap.

How upset is my cappuccino,

I dream of running fingers through

The juice of nature that flows like Zimbabwe's Victoria Falls.

As I touch your pussy cat,

Aroma flavour swims with muscle,

Gentle kisses reach breathless…

Indulge in passion, champagne, wine and liquor,

Lips to lick off drips,

Juicier, oh ooooh, oooooooh,

Paradise awaiting in ecstasy.

Oh, you make me feel horny – babe,

Let cappuccino melt within me.

Are you feeling me?

Chapter Eight

Love Is Truly Blind

Closer Moment

As I gaze at your eyes, I see myself,

Falling with a stranger who is no other than you – darling,

You're the one saturating my mind with the rising and set of the sun.

I am under your spell of warmth and embrace,

You're kind, compassionate, sincere, elegant, gentle and precious.

Closer I look, deeper I find the beauty of love.

You're to me as Catherine to Heathcliff in a positive sense.

Don't let the flame go out until the battle is won.

As I hold you in my arms,

My lips tremble and long to smother you from head to toe.

I must control myself as nature rises.

The thought of being with you, alone, is like heaven right here on earth,

I miss your mind each day,

I see your face overlooking my shadow.

M25 Romantic Jammin

I think about you romantically in traffic.

I think about your presence, how you seduced my mind to think of you only.

You intoxicate my lips to kiss you,

My eyes see no one but you,

My heart craves for your warmth,

I feel sentimental when I see your picture.

I cannot help myself, until I rest my weary soul upon you.

You are the light of my heart,

You are my past, present and future.

All I do is for us to be happy,

Although, this happiness takes two.

I know what it means to be happy inside and out.

I know what it means to be sad without tears.

Distant memories provoke thoughts of yesterday.

I love myself just as I love those who are neglected.

Through my pain I learned to listen and understand.

I help those who deserve helping.

I cast away arrogance and welcome humility.

I love life and I love those who hate me for me.

I love always.

Violeta

Silvery, shining star, you are.

Your walk is like a perfect tiger.

Elegantly you sway from side to side,

Eyes fill with the twinkle of magic,

Smile that seduces lips into thoughtless tenderness.

Beauty Of Monterrey

How sweet is your voice, like singing birds,

Sounds of peace and warmth.

I picture your smile, like a half moon,

I imagine your eyes, like stars filled with sparkles,

I envision your cheeks like pink apple blossom,

I long to hold you in my arms and sprinkle kisses with smiles.

Romantic Tale of Afreurop

As I thought about our brief moments together by Neuchatel Lake,

My heart yearned for your wholeness.

How selfish can love be?

Without selfishness, there are no feelings of togetherness,

And wanting to share provocative thoughts.

I understand not why I feel this way, but I care about you.

Although, I know nothing of you,

Your trembling voice conveys compassion and ethical essence I admire.

I promise you laughter, love of everlasting romance and not of convenience,

Please take me in your adorable arms, as the sky holds the cloud.

I'm missing you.

Exercise

My heart-strings weaken and pull like a swinging pendulum,

Slight stretches drench pain through my upper body.

Mind, thoughtless it becomes,

searching for that healthy appetite,

Night fly-away and cloud wandering in,

Yet another day, and effortlessly I remain in my rocking chair with wine floating before my eyes.

Maria

You walk like a cheetah,

Elegance at its best,

Your eyes like gleaming sunset,

Your smile seduces me and captures devoted attention,

Your gentle words whisper like sea breezes,

Beauty of your rainbow belongs to the sky.

How can I be your possession?

Neuchatel Lake

Standing still I gaze at the wave;

You cruise away without looking back.

Your affection seems pointless because you're rippling my mind with waves of your thoughts,

Alps, green fields vanish into clouds that I can no longer see,

How could you stare at me with your invisible eyes?

I miss you,

Peace and cool breezes penetrate my mind with memories.

Once more I miss you.

La Mia Stanzetta (My Room)

Since you've left, our season of love unveils memories of togetherness,

Pictures of your true, loving heart naturally descend upon my universe

Like shining stars.

Your presence radiates light of colourful butterflies,

Beauty with elegance and such captivating mind of intelligence,

This softens and surrenders me into your precious, gentle arms;

Arms covered with warmth and comfort,

Embracing one's thoughts and desires.

Taiwanese Hero

In foreign land I feel your closeness, warmth and comfort,

But the suffering within is greater than the joy I seek,

The laughter vanishes like smoke.

No hero I dare speak of.

Hero within, please come to me and uplift your sorrow,

Your moment of anguish, and disappear; draw nearer.

But when I hold you in my thought,

It's like the wind embracing the sea wave, causing it to roar with affection,

Expressing togetherness in spells of high and low, like those of hill plain and valley,

Always and forever be still within, with love and understanding.

Un Bel Posto
(Beautiful Place)

As I write this poem,

Sun sets behind the mountains of beautiful Nervi,

Sea waves roar and embrace the storming wind,

Defenceless rocks express signs of compassionate love.

Damascus

Mellow, mellow,

What an old city with charismatic nature.

Buildings, rocky mountains shake the soil beneath.

Watered land, far from green grass.

I feel heat and seduction of warmth that intoxicates my throat.

Surroundings high and low display the history of existence,

So sincere are the people, many struggle and many quit,

Troublesome past whither into darkness.

Children loved by Supreme Being.

Future seems in disarray at present, but I yearn for hope and joy.

I depart like a seasonal bird.

I return with love and moments of pleasure.

Chapter Nine

Immune System To Sickness And Death

Smiling Soul

Many tears will fall.

Many tears will dry just like the rain.

The breeze carries the emotions, the feeling of loss.

Cloud looms over sky with sorrows that reflect temporary moments.

Suddenly, tears dry by the gentle wind

For a moment smile was afar

I reminisce through the days of yesterday's memories.

The sun rises and shines through the sky.

My life is the joy beyond words.

My life has been wonderful with many friends over the years

My loving friends and family are wondering about how I am doing;

I am doing fine.

I wish you could all see me now.

I am fit to walk,

Fit to laugh,

Fit to take a bath by myself, not that you need one up here.

I thank you for the love that you gave during the good and sad times.

Battling With Hay Fever

Don't you see redness of my eyes?

Yes, summer it may be for those who long to enjoy the sunniest day.

As for me, lonely I sneeze in agony,

Colourful they look but with itchiness that blitz my eye lids,

Sorer they become with sleeping eyes, as I awake.

Nose bleed irritates like crazy,

Throat gusts like a tornado.

Restless I become as the medicine works within,

Drowsiness draws closer.

Tickle eyes like a tired baby craving sleep, with wet nose like Lassie,

Although season is wonderful.

How much longer can I suffer this hay fever?

My immune systems weaken and expose to El Niño effect.

I suffered not when in beautiful Africa.

I reside across the sea, quickly I adapt to new life.

I lost my identify because secrets of cultures dwell within.

Let no one tell you different; believe in your strength and weakness.

Your weakness is your strength when you nurture it.

Cancer Season

Alone I search high and low for inspiration.

Alone I sit here staring at four lonely walls,

Alone I endure one of life's growths,

But you're compassionate, abounding in love.

You're the reason why I must go on.

But let not your worries trouble you,

Life is your chariot.

Think of me not until you're through.

You hold the key of laughter, sadness and joy.

I will be with you day or night,

As long you hold me in your thoughts - be strong.

Notes

Made in the USA
Charleston, SC
05 May 2013